Colour Yourself to
TRANQUILLITY

AND REDUCE STRESS WITH THESE BEAUTIFUL ARTWORKS OF TREES

ORIGINAL ART BY
Melissa Launay

CICO BOOKS
LONDON NEW YORK

Published in 2017 by CICO Books
An imprint of Ryland Peters & Small Ltd
20–21 Jockey's Fields   341 E 116th St
London WC1R 4BW   New York, NY 10029

www.rylandpeters.com

10 9 8 7 6 5 4 3 2 1

Design, text, and illustration © CICO Books 2017

The author's moral rights have been asserted. All rights reserved. No part of this publication may be reproduced, stored in a retrieval system, or transmitted in any form or by any means, electronic, mechanical, photocopying, or otherwise, without the prior permission of the publisher.

A CIP catalog record for this book is available from the Library of Congress and the British Library.

US ISBN: 978-1-78249-448-5
(*Color Yourself to Tranquility*)

UK ISBN: 978-1-78249-420-1
(*Colour Yourself to Tranquillity*)

Printed in China

Senior editor: Carmel Edmonds
Designer: Jerry Goldie
Art director: Sally Powell
Head of production: Patricia Harrington
Publishing manager: Penny Craig
Publisher: Cindy Richards

About the artist
Melissa Launay lives and works in Malaga, Spain. She achieved an MA in Fine Art from the University of Seville and has illustrated several books for British and American publishers, including *Be More Tree* for CICO Books.

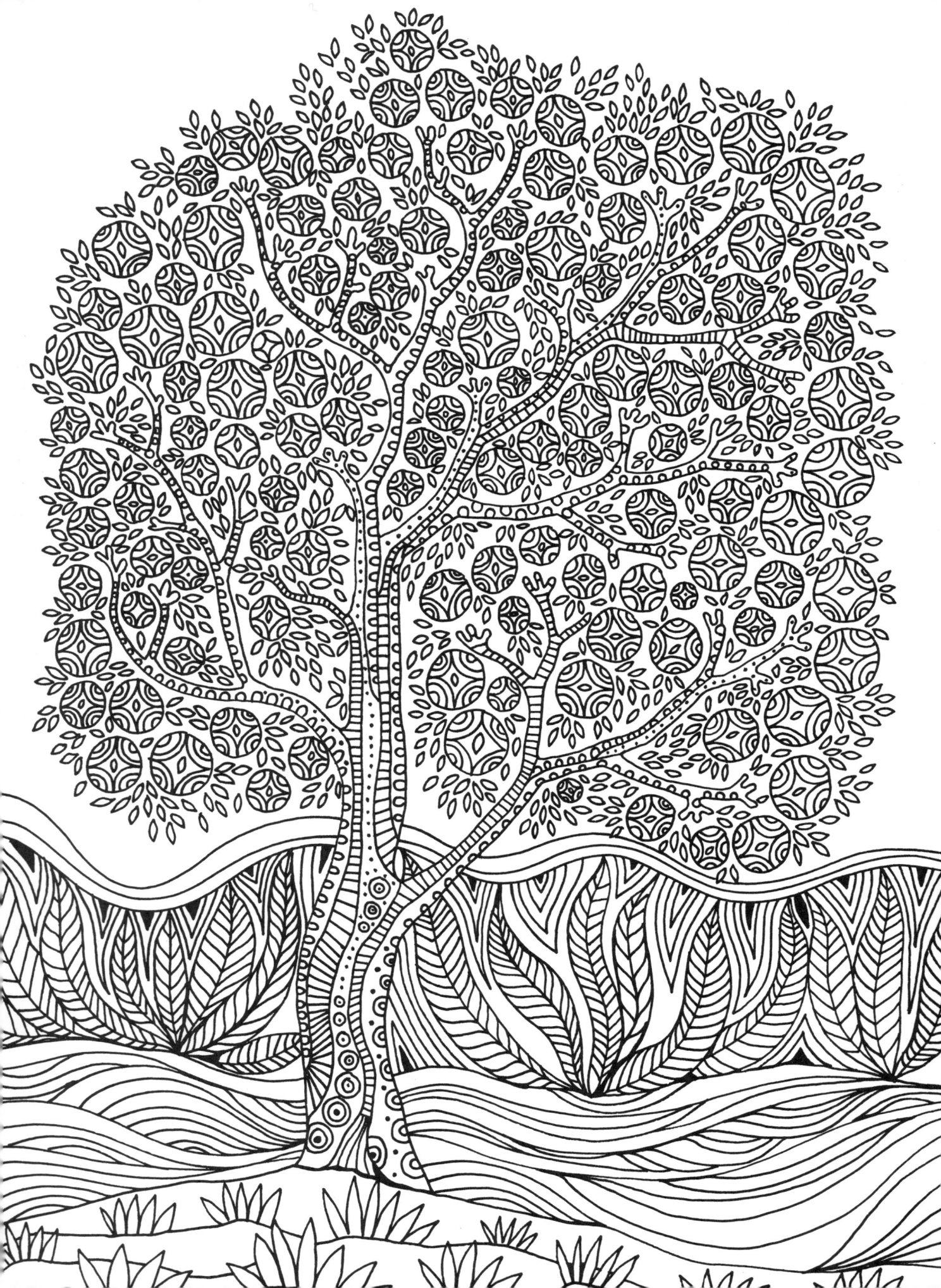

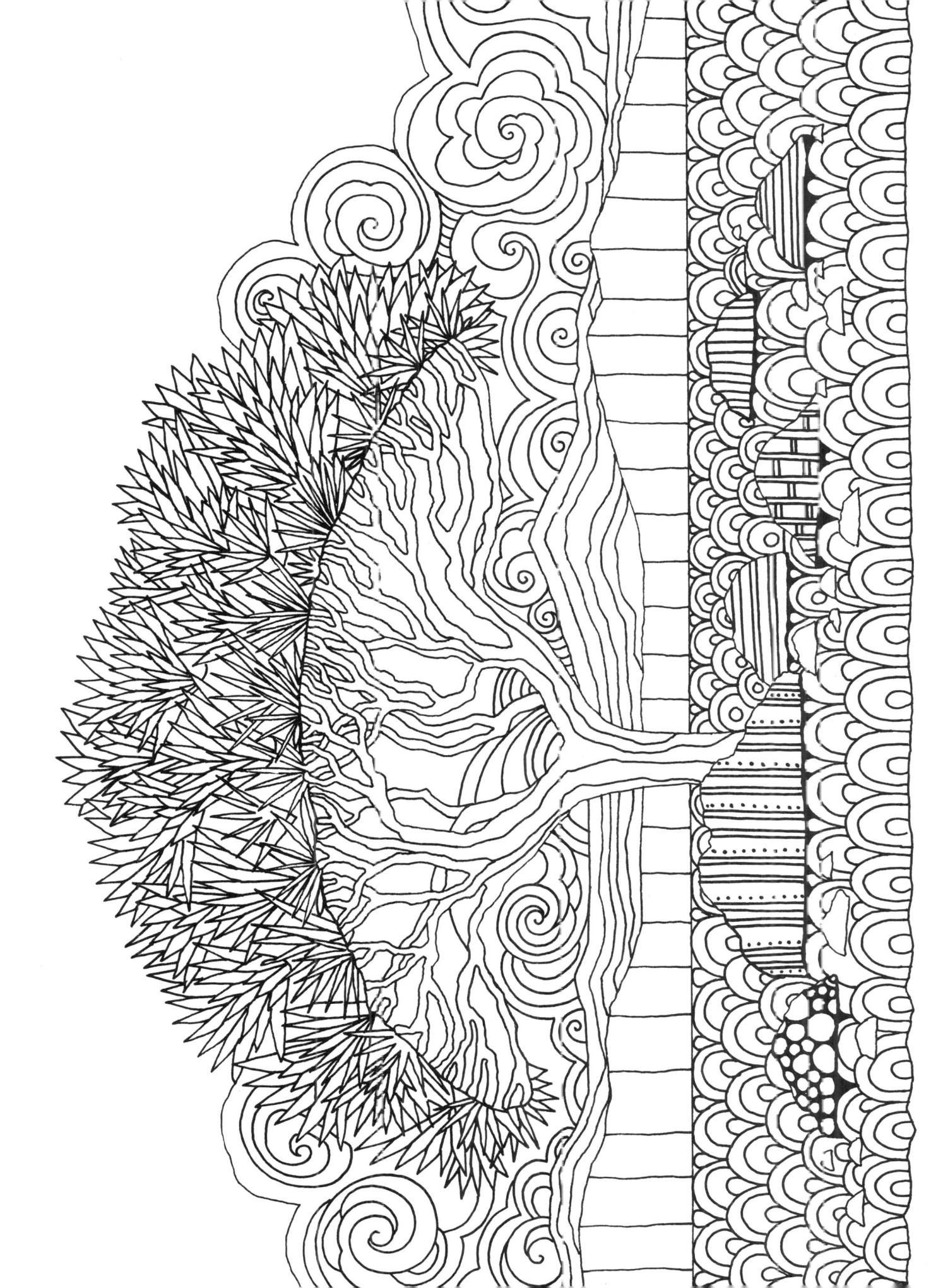

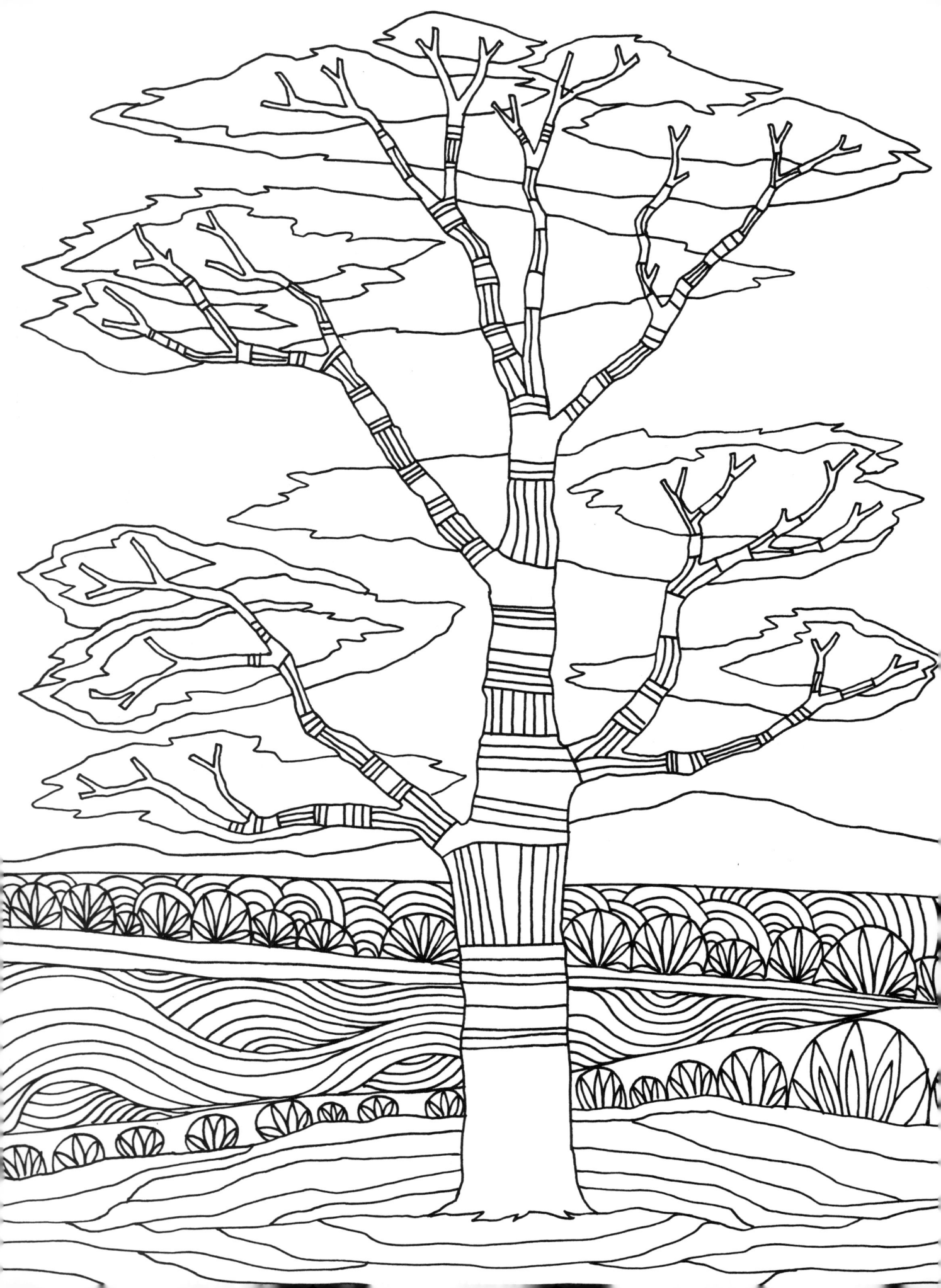

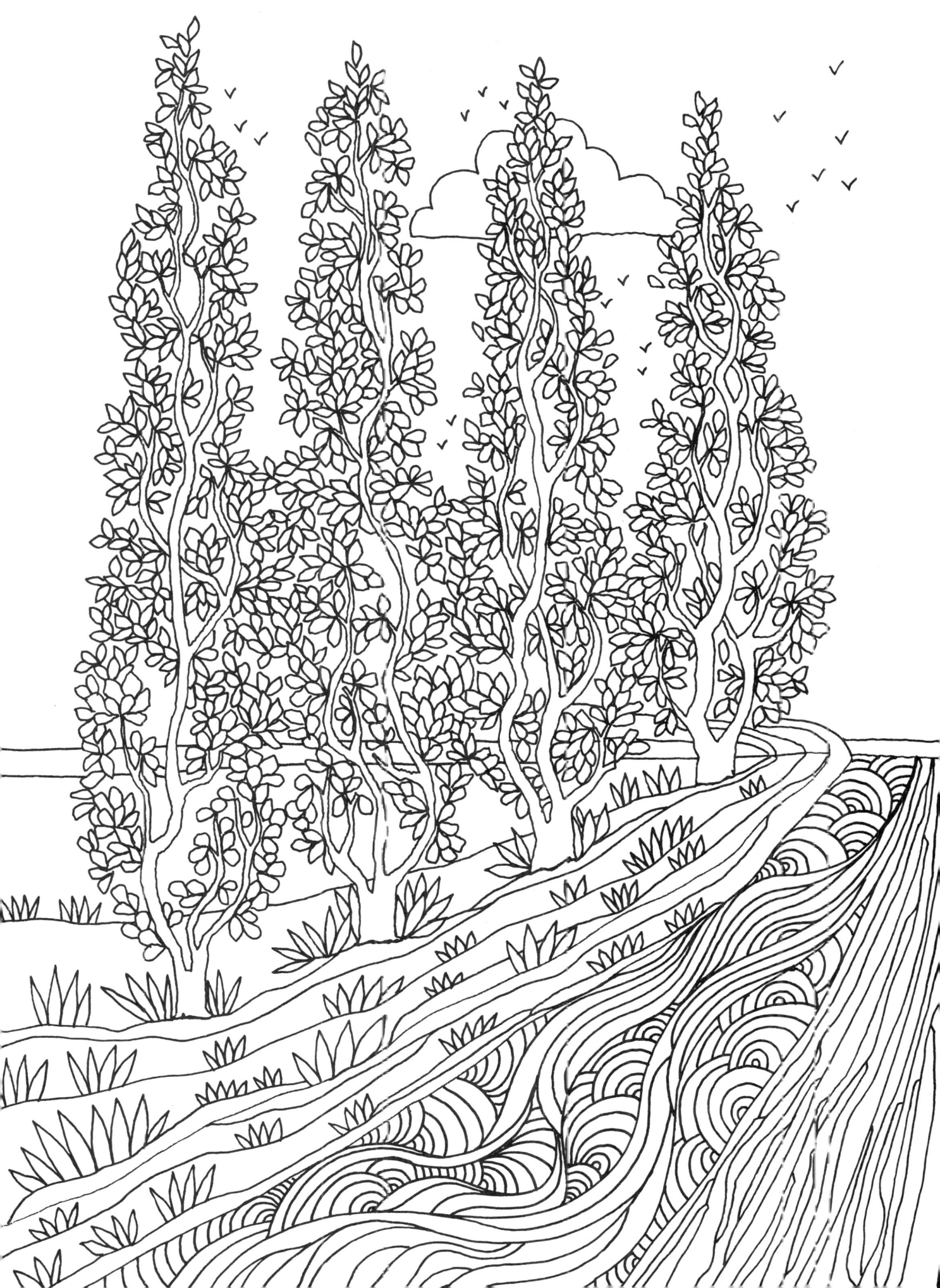

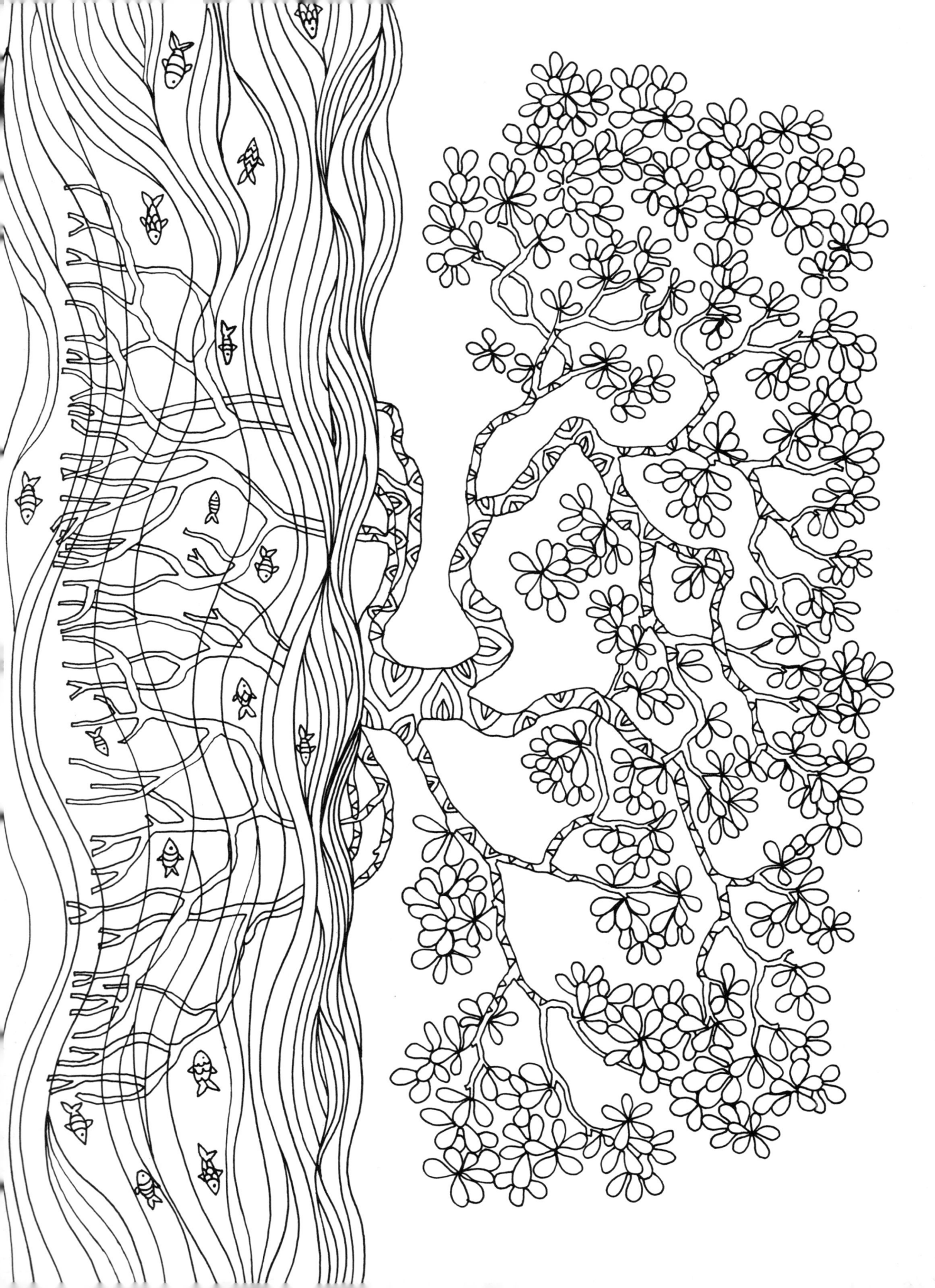